AROUND TOWN
MUSE...

CW00819746

by Adeline J. Zimmerman

TABLE OF CONTENTS

WORDS TO KNOW

art

bones

bugs

learn

museum

science

MUSEUM

Let's go to the museum!

butterfly

We see bugs.

dinosaur
bones

We see bones.

We see science.

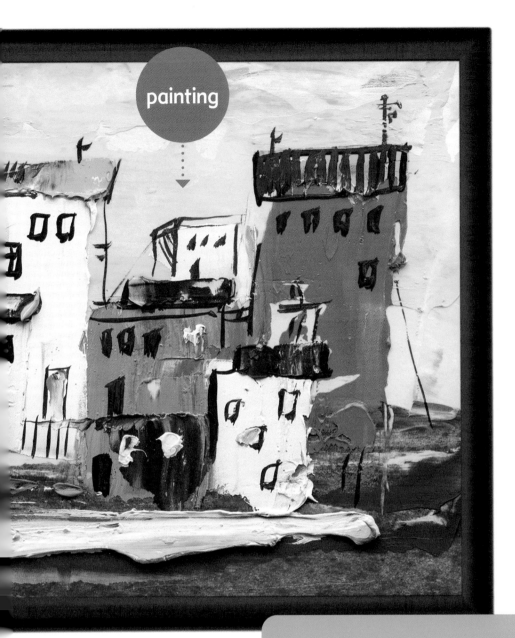

painting

We see art.

We learn.

We play!

LET'S REVIEW!

What are these kids learning about at the museum?

INDEX